40 Ways in 40 Days

40 Ways in 40 Days

A GUIDE TO PRAYER

DARREN CUSHMAN WOOD

North United Methodist Church • Indianapolis, IN

© 2022 North United Methodist Church, 3808 N. Meridian St., Indianapolis, IN 46208. NorthChurchIndy.com.

ISBN 978-1-7327761-1-1 (epub)

ISBN 978-1-7327761-0-4 (paperback)

The cover art comes from a small portion of one of the many beautiful banners throughout North United Methodist Church created by the late Doris Douglas, a long-time member, and other artists.

Biblical quotations from the New Revised Standard Version of the Bible, copyright © 1989 by the Division of Christian Education of the National Council of the Churches of Christ in the USA and used by permission.

Hymn quotations from The United Methodist Hymnal, copyright © 1989 by the United Methodist Publishing House and from The Faith We Sing, copyright © 2000 by Abingdon Press and used by permission.

Contents

Introduction   1

Part I. Main Body

1. Dirty Devotion   5
2. The Daily Office (Lauds and Vespers)   7
3. You Are a Character   9
4. Work Prayer   11
5. Palms Down, Palms Up   13
6. The Lord's Prayer Outline   15
7. Three Times a Day   17
8. Caim Prayer   19
9. Body Prayer Confession   21
10. Daily Examen   23
11. Breath Prayer One   25
12. All-Day Lord's Prayer   27

13.	Slacker Prayer	29
14.	Prayers for the World	31
15.	Lectio Divina	33
16.	A Lectionary Day	35
17.	The Jesus Prayer	37
18.	The Lord's Prayer With Music	39
19.	Wall of Prayer	41
20.	Canticle of the Sun	43
21.	Praying Psalm 37:4	47
22.	Prayer Walk	49
23.	"Here I Am" Prayer	51
24.	Paraphrase The Lord's Prayer	53
25.	Hymn for the Day	55
26.	Prayers for the Dead	57
27.	Pushing Your Buttons	59
28.	Materialist Meditation	61
29.	Wandering Prayer	63
30.	Moving to The Lord's Prayer	65
31.	Write Your Own Psalm	67
32.	Peace Prayer	69

33.	Reconciliation By Water or Fire	71
34.	Audiebant Divina	73
35.	Meditation on an Image	75
36.	Praying with Incense	77
37.	Divine Letter	79
38.	Five Senses Prayer	81
39.	Fasting or Abstinence	83
40.	Day of Simplicity, Silence, and Light	85
41.	Lenten Supplemental Exercises	89
	About the Author	97

Introduction

INTRODUCTION

What is prayer? Henri Nouwen, an internationally known priest and author, defined prayer in many different ways:[1]

- "To pray means to think and live in the presence of God."
- "Prayer is the way to let the life-giving Spirit of God penetrate all the corners of my being."
- "Prayer is the act by which we divest ourselves of all false belongings and become free to belong to God and God alone."
- "To pray means to stop expecting from God the same small-mindedness which you discover in yourself."
- "Prayer means letting God's creative love touch the most hidden places of our being and letting Jesus' way of the cross truly become our way."

The list of definitions could go on, but suffice it to say the enormity of prayer can leave us wondering how to do it.

40W/40D

This guidebook will help you discover practical ways to pray that will draw you closer to God. It includes 40 different ways to pray that can be done over 40 days—40W/40D. While this process was originally designed for Lent, these exercises can be done any time of the year.

Since there are different kinds of temperaments and multiple forms of intelligences, we need a variety of ways to approach prayer. This guidebook offers different types of prayers using a variety of approaches—silent reflection, writing, drawing, singing and dancing. Some of the prayers will feel comfortable but others will feel awkward. Try them all to see which ones work for you.

TWO WAYS TO USE THIS BOOK

There are two ways to use this guidebook.

A Season of Prayer: You can use it during a planned 40-day season such as Lent. It can easily be adapted for a congregation-wide study of prayer and a sermon series on prayer, such as a series on each line in the Lord's Prayer. Whether you use it as an individual, with a small group, or in leading an entire congregation, this is a step-by-step process for deepening and expanding your understanding of prayer. The simpler exercises are at the beginning of the process and progress to longer, more complex ones. This way you will develop your "spiritual stamina" as the season goes along.

Roughly speaking, there is a flow to each week:
- Sundays—public worship;
- Mondays—centering prayers;

- Tuesdays—the Lord's Prayer;
- Wednesdays—prayers of adoration and thanksgiving;
- Thursdays—prayers of intercession;
- Fridays—prayers of confession and petition, and
- Saturdays—contemplation.

Because some of the prayers require advance planning, on Sundays be sure to review all the exercises for a week. Here is a sample schedule based on Lent (from Ash Wednesday to Holy Saturday):

Sunday	Monday	Tuesday	Wednesday	Thursday	Friday	Saturday
			#1 Dirty Devotion	#2 Lauds or Vespers	#3 You Are a Character	#4 Work Prayer
Public Worship	#5 Palms Down, Palms Up	#6 Lord's Prayer Outline	#7 Three Times a Day	#8 Calm Prayer	#9 Body Prayer of Confession	#10 Daily Examen
Public Worship	#11 Breath Prayer One	#12 Lord's Prayer All Day	#13 Slacker Prayer	#14 Prayers for the World	#15 Lectio Divina	#16 A Lectionary Day
Public Worship	#17 Jesus Prayer	#18 Lord's Prayer with Music	#19 Wall of Prayer	#20 Canticle of the Sun	#21 Praying Psalm	#22 Prayer Walk
Public Worship	#23 I Am Here	#24 Lord's Prayer Paraphrase	#25 Hymn for the Day	#26 Prayers for the Dead	#27 Pushing Your Buttons	#28 Materialist Meditation
Public Worship	#29 Wandering Prayer	#30 Moving to the Lord's Prayer	#31 Write Your Psalm	#32 Peace Prayer	#33 Water/Fire Reconciliation	#34 Audiebant Divina
Public Worship	#35 Meditation on an Image	#36 Praying with Incense	#37 Divine Letter	#38 Five Senses Prayer	#39 Fasting and Abstinence	#40 Simplicity, Silence and Light

À La Carte: You can randomly select the prayer exercises. Think of this guidebook as a box of recipes that provide a step-by-step guide to different forms of prayer.

Each prayer exercise was designed to be done in a single day (except for the two-day fasting/abstinence exercise). They are for individual use but can be adapted to be done with others. Some of them are very short (less than a minute), and others require more time (such as 30 minutes). And like a recipe, feel free to adapt them to your temperament and needs.

1 "The Only Necessary Thing" compiled and edited by Wendy Wilson Greer.

1. Dirty Devotion

PURPOSE: TO REMIND US THAT WE ARE CREATURES WHO ARE DEPENDENT ON GOD

Genuine prayer is based on honesty with God and ourselves that puts us in touch with our limitations and makes us grateful for our creator. This exercise involves our bodies as well as our minds in centering us in the presence of our maker.

Step 1: Get some dirt.

Step 2: Put your hands in the dirt and play with it. You may want to get some seeds or a sprout and plant it in the dirt.

Step 3: As you work your hands in the dirt or mud, remember Genesis 2:7, "Then the Lord God formed the human from the dust of the ground, and breathed into his nostrils the breath of life, and the human became a living being."

Step 4: Meditate on how every dimension of your life and every breath you take are wholly dependent on God.

Step 5: Give God thanks for all the gifts God has given you to sustain and protect you.

Step 6: Wash your hands!

2. The Daily Office (Lauds and Vespers)

PURPOSE: BEGIN OR END YOUR DAY WITH PRAYERS AND SCRIPTURE READINGS

Known by various names ("canonical hours," "divine office," "liturgy of the hours") the "daily office" divides the day into fixed periods of prayer. All major Christian traditions have versions of it and divide the day in various ways. The two most familiar times for prayer are lauds (morning) and vespers (evening), with shorter periods of prayer throughout the day and night. There are particular psalms and canticles that are traditionally used for these times of prayer.

There are many different versions of the daily office. A simple format that draws from readings traditionally used within these hours follows.

Morning (Lauds)	Evening (Vespers)
Opening Sentence: O Lord, let my soul rise to meet you as the day rises to meet the sun.	**Opening Sentence:** Light and peace in Jesus Christ. Thanks be to God.
A Morning Psalm: 3, 5, 30, 59, 88, 92, 95, 100 or 130	**An Evening Psalm:** 67, 88, 90, 91, 98, 121, 134, 136 or 139
Silence	
Read Luke 1:68-79	**Read** Luke 1:46-55 or 2:29-32
Gloria Patri: Glory be to the Father, and to the Son, and to the Holy Ghost; as it was in the beginning, is now and ever shall be, world without end. Amen.	**Doxology:** Praise God, from whom all blessings flow; Praise God, all creatures here below; Praise God, above, all heavenly host; Praise Father, Son, and Holy Ghost. Amen.
Prayers of Intercession for Others	
Prayer of Thanksgiving	
Benediction: Christ within me, Christ beneath me, Christ above me, Christ to my right side, Christ to my left, Christ in his breadth, Christ in his length, Christ in his depth, Christ in the heart of all who think of me, Christ in the mouth of all who speak of me, Christ in every eye that sees me, Christ in every ear that hears me. I arise today in a mighty strength, making in my mouth the trinity, believing in my mind three persons, confessing in my heart they are one, thanking my creator. (From St. Patrick's "Lorica")	**Benediction:** I lie down this night with God, and God will lie down with me; I lie down this night with Christ, and Christ will lie down with me; I lie down this night with the Spirit, and the Spirit will lie down with me; God and Christ and the Spirit be lying down with me. (From the "Carmina Gadelica")

3. You Are a Character

PURPOSE: USE YOUR IMAGINATION TO PRAY WITH SCRIPTURE

Step 1: Select a short- to medium-length story in the Bible (such as Genesis 12:1-9, Exodus 14:10-25, Matthew 14:22-33, Mark 6:30-44 or Acts 16:16-34). Read the story.

Step 2: Read the story a second time. Pause periodically and imagine: What you see? What you hear? What you smell?

Step 3: Select one of the characters in the story and read it a third time while replacing your name for theirs. Imagine yourself as that character. How do you react? How do you feel?

Step 4: With an awareness of God's presence through the scripture passage, begin to pray.

4. Work Prayer

PURPOSE: SEE MANUAL TASKS AS PRAYER

Brother Lawrence was a lay member of a Carmelite monastery in Paris in the 1600s. Although he never wrote, the abbot of the monastery recorded their conversations about prayer. Brother Lawrence once described manual labor this way: "We ought not to be weary of doing little things for the love of God, who regards not the greatness of the work, but the love with which it is performed."

Step 1: Select a manual task such as washing dishes, folding towels or shoveling dirt.

Step 2: Before you begin the task, make the sign of the cross and say, "In the name of the Father and of the Son and of the Holy Spirit" or "In the name of the Holy Trinity" to express that during this moment you are intentionally becoming aware that you and all creation live within the very life of God, whose being is a dynamic relationship of eternal love.

Step 3: Do the task as an act of prayer, being aware that everything you do is done to the glory of God and is a channel through which the Holy Spirit comes to you.

Step 4: After the task is completed or your time has come to an end, offer a prayer such as the Lord's Prayer.

How to Make the Sign of the Cross
Using your right hand, you should touch your forehead at the mention of the Father; the lower middle of your chest at the mention of the Son; the left shoulder on the word "Holy" and the right shoulder on the word "Spirit." (This is the Western version—Catholic, Lutheran, Episcopalian, etc. The Eastern or Orthodox version goes from right to left and the fingers are held so as to represent the Trinity and the two natures of Christ.)

---

5. Palms Down, Palms Up

PURPOSE: CENTERING ONESELF IN THE PRESENCE OF GOD

Step 1: Remove as many distractions as possible. Take several slow, deep breaths.

Step 2: Hold your hands palms down and envision giving all your burdens *to* God. Imagine these things falling out of your hands.

Step 3: When you can imagine your hands empty, turn your hands palms up and think about what you need *from* God. Imagine God putting those things into your hands.

Step 4: Close by saying, "So be it. Amen."

6. The Lord's Prayer Outline

PURPOSE: USE THE LORD'S PRAYER AS A BASIC OUTLINE FOR PRAYER

Step 1 (Adoration): Say "Our Father, who art in heaven, hallowed be thy name." Address God with various titles and names that are meaningful to you. Offer God praise.

Step 2 (Intercession): Say "Thy kingdom come, thy will be done, on earth, as it is in heaven." Offer prayers of intercession for the world and individuals who are in need.

Step 3 (Petition): Say "Give us this day our daily bread." Share your needs with God.

Step 4 (Confession): Say "Forgive us our trespasses as we forgive those who trespass against us. And lead us not into temptation but deliver us from evil." Confess your sins to God and ask for God's help for the day.

Step 5 (Thanksgiving): Thank God for what God has

done for you. End your prayer with "For thine is the kingdom and the power and the glory forever. Amen."

7. Three Times a Day

PURPOSE: PRAY THREE TIMES TODAY

Based on Daniel 6:10, there is an old tradition in Christianity of facing east and praying three times a day. Facing east is based on the Natal Star shining in the eastern sky at Jesus' birth and the hope of the second coming of Christ from the east (Matthew 24:27). This exercise will help you develop a daily rhythm of short prayers to mark your day.

Decide in advance the three times of the day you will pause for prayer. These moments are very short; just a couple of minutes. However, be sure you will not be interrupted. Each time follow this outline:
- Make the sign of the cross and say, "In the name of the Father and of the Son and of the Holy Spirit" or "In the name of the Holy Trinity" to express that during this moment you are intentionally becoming aware that you live every moment within the very

life of God, whose being is a dynamic relationship of eternal love that includes you.

- Read a short selection of scripture (one to three verses).
- Offer a short prayer of petition asking God to help you or someone else.
- Conclude with a short prayer of praise and thanksgiving.

Feel free to add to this outline. For example, reading from a devotional such as "The Upper Room," singing a hymn, or saying the Lord's Prayer.

8. Caim Prayer

PURPOSE: HOW TO PRAY FOR OTHERS WHEN YOU DO NOT KNOW WHAT TO PRAY

Caim or "encircling" prayer comes from the Celtic tradition and can be adapted for many different situations when praying for another person. The invisible circle symbolizes the love of God encircling the person.

The following three examples come from "Celtic Daily Prayer" from the Northumbria Community, an intentional Christian community in Northern England that practices the Celtic tradition:

With your finger, draw a circle clockwise around yourself as you say one of these prayers:

Circle [name], Lord.
Keep protection near and danger afar.
Keep peace within and turmoil out. Amen.

God, circle [name].

Keep home within; keep despair away. Amen.

[Name], the compassing of the Sacred Three be upon you.
The compassing of the Sacred Three protect you.
The compassing of the Sacred Three preserve you. Amen.

9. Body Prayer Confession

PURPOSE: USE GESTURES TO CONFESS YOUR SINS

Step 1: Make fists. Think about all the ways you have disobeyed or distanced yourself from God.

Step 2: Open your hands. Offer your sins to God, asking God to forgive you and free you from all sin.

Step 3: Cup your hands. Spend several moments focusing on God's forgiveness and acceptance of you.

Step 4: Place your hands together in front of your heart. Give God thanks.

10. Daily Examen

PURPOSE: PRAYERFULLY REVIEW THE EVENTS OF THE DAY

The practice of a daily examen ("examination") comes from the Ignatian tradition (Jesuits) in Roman Catholicism. An examen is a series of reflection questions and prayers normally done at the close of the day. There are a variety of examens, some quite elaborate. This version comes from United Methodist Bishop Sharon Brown Christopher:

Step 1: Give God thanks for the day and for God's presence.

Step 2: Reflect on these questions:
- Where did I notice the presence of God today?
- What do I need to confess?
- Whom do I need to forgive?
- For what do I give thanks?
- What has God taught me today?

Step 3: Name the day.

Step 4: Identify the gift(s) needed for tomorrow.

Step 5: Offer your life back to God. Let go of all troubling thoughts and concerns about the day.

11. Breath Prayer One

PURPOSE: TO FOLLOW BREATHING AS IT LEADS TO GOD

A breath prayer is a short petition or praise in rhythm with your breathing that helps you become aware of God's presence. In this version a short phrase or scripture verse is used. The first half is said or thought as you inhale and the second half is said or thought as you exhale. Here are a few sample phrases:
- Be still and know that I am God.
- Lord, have mercy.
- The Lord is my light and my salvation.
- Not my will, but yours.
- Come, Holy Spirit.

Step 1: Determine the amount of time you will designate for your breath prayer.

Step 2: Settle into a comfortable position and begin to slow down your breathing. Take long, deep breaths and relax your body.

Step 3: You may want to close your eyes as you silently recall the phrase. Slowly sync your inhalation and exhalation with the parts of the phrase. Do not analyze or interpret the phrase. Don't repress or scrutinize your thoughts but let them pass through your mind. Simply be in God's presence.

Step 4: Slowly come to the end of meditating on the phrase and open your eyes.

12. All-Day Lord's Prayer

PURPOSE: MEDITATE ON THE LORD'S PRAYER THROUGHOUT THE DAY

Use the Lord's Prayer as a series of *short* meditations woven throughout your day. At certain times of the day, pause for a moment and pray a line from the prayer and then reflect on its meaning for a few minutes, or, if your type of work allows, reflect on it while you perform your tasks. Let the phrase be the theme for the next part of your day. If needed, set the alarm on your phone or computer to remind you to move on to the next line.

For example, the following breakdown is for 30-minute intervals during an eight-hour day.

9 a.m. — Our Father
9:30 a.m. — in heaven,
10 a.m. — hallowed be your name,
10:30 a.m. — your kingdom come,

11 a.m.— your will be done
11:30 a.m. — on earth as in heaven.
12 p.m. — Give us today our daily bread.
12:30 p.m. — Forgive us our sins
1 p.m. — as we forgive those who sin against us.
1:30 p.m. — Save us from the time of trial
2 p.m. — and deliver us from evil.
2:30 p.m. — For the kingdom,
3 p.m. — the power,
3:30 p.m. — and the glory
4 p.m. — are yours, now and forever.
4:30 p.m. — Amen.

If it helps, print off the Lord's Prayer and keep it with you, and after you have finished meditating on a line cross it off.

13. Slacker Prayer

PURPOSE: MAKE PRAYER PART OF YOUR ORDINARY ROUTINE

Step 1: Pause from your work. Remain silent and still for 30 seconds. Say silently, "In the name of the Father and of the Son and of the Holy Spirit" or "In the name of the Holy Trinity" to express that during this moment you are intentionally becoming aware you and all creation live within the very life of God, whose being is a dynamic relationship of eternal love.

Step 2: Look at the things at hand and the task you are performing. Remember God is present. Dedicate your work to God.

Step 3: Look at the people around you. Remember they are created in God's image. Give God thanks for them and pray for their wellbeing.

Step 4: Then continue what you were doing as a prayer, doing everything for the glory of God.

14. Prayers for the World

PURPOSE: ORGANIZE YOUR PRAYERS OF INTERCESSION

In preparation for this exercise you may want to read or watch the news and make a list of a variety of concerns and issues.

Step 1: Begin your prayers with a title or attribute for God (e.g. "Great Sovereign," "Loving Creator," "Wise Judge"). Begin each intercession with, "Hear my prayers for...."

Step 2: Name the concerns in your neighborhood.

Step 3: Name the concerns in your city and county.

Step 4: Name the concerns in your state.

Step 5: Name the concerns in your nation.

Step 6: Name the concerns around the world.

Step 7: Conclude with this doxology:

> Praise God from whom all blessings flow.
> Praise God all creatures here below.

Praise the Sovereign, Savior and Spirit forever more. Amen.

15. Lectio Divina

PURPOSE: EXPLORE HOW SCRIPTURE LEADS TO PRAYER

Lectio divina, or "divine reading," developed in the medieval monasteries as a part of the Daily Office. It begins with reading aloud (lectio) that leads to pondering its meaning (meditatio) which, in turn, gives way to prayers (oratio) so that the individual spends the rest of the day in the presence of God (contemplatio).

Step 1: Select a scripture text of no more than 10 verses, such as one (or part of one) of the following: (Psalm 1, Isaiah 11:6-9, Matthew 4:18-22, Luke 10:38-42 or Romans 8:12-17).

Step 2: Read the passage aloud. Say the word or phrase that catches your attention. Do not analyze it or try to interpret it.

Step 3: Read the passage aloud a second time. Ask yourself, "What does this passage reveal about God?"

Step 4: Read the passage aloud a third time. Ask yourself, "Based on the passage, what does God want me to do or to be?"

Step 5: With an awareness of God's presence through the scripture passage, begin to pray.

16. A Lectionary Day

PURPOSE: USE THE LECTIONARY AS A DAY OF PRAYER

The lectionary is a cycle of readings for every Sunday of the year that follows the church calendar. Each Sunday there are four readings: an Old Testament lesson, an Epistle lesson, a Psalm, and a Gospel lesson. Different traditions have different lectionaries that will vary somewhat. The one used by most Protestants is the "Revised Common Lectionary," which you can find online.

You can use the four lectionary readings as a format for prayer throughout a single day:
- Morning—Old Testament lesson;
- Noon—Epistle lesson;
- Evening—Gospel lesson, and
- Bedtime—Psalm.

Before each reading, pause and ask the Holy Spirit to open your heart and mind to speak to you through the scriptures. After each reading conclude by saying, "This is the word of God for the people of God, thanks be to God."

17. The Jesus Prayer

PURPOSE: CENTER ONESELF IN THE PRESENCE OF GOD BY REPEATING THIS TRADITIONAL PRAYER

The "Jesus Prayer" is one of the oldest and most famous prayers in Christianity. Based on Luke 18:13 and Mark 10:47, it is a type of breath prayer. It is prominent in the Orthodox tradition as a way to practice deep contemplation of the heart.

Step 1: Determine how long you will spend with this prayer and the setting that is best for you. Some may want to do this seated quietly. Others may want to engage in an activity such as walking, bike riding, or working in the garden.

Step 2: Begin repeating the Jesus Prayer:

"Lord Jesus Christ, Son of God, have mercy on me, a sinner."

Step 3: After some time has passed, emphasize each

important word or phrase in order as you repeat the prayer, meditating on the significance of each:

"*Lord* Jesus Christ, Son of God, have mercy on me, a sinner."

"Lord *Jesus* Christ, Son of God, have mercy on me, a sinner."

"Lord Jesus *Christ*, Son of God, have mercy on me, a sinner."

"Lord Jesus Christ, *Son* of God, have mercy on me, a sinner."

"Lord Jesus Christ, Son *of God*, have mercy on me, a sinner."

"Lord Jesus Christ, Son of God, *have mercy* on me, a sinner."

"Lord Jesus Christ, Son of God, have mercy *on me*, a sinner."

"Lord Jesus Christ, Son of God, have mercy on me, *a sinner*."

Step 4: End with a moment of silence.

18. The Lord's Prayer With Music

PURPOSE: MEDITATE ON THE MEANING OF THE LORD'S PRAYER

The Lord's Prayer has been set to music in a variety of ways. It can be sung or chanted. There are many different recordings of it. Spend today periodically singing or listening to the Lord's Prayer. Try singing it to a tune you have heard during the day. Allow the music to help you pray. Before you go to sleep, listen to it or sing it one last time.

19. Wall of Prayer

PURPOSE: USE ART TO EXPRESS YOUR PRAYERS

Step 1: At the beginning of the day, obtain a large piece of paper or posterboard. Write the following headings for different types of prayer (in an arrangement of your choosing):
- Adoration (prayers of praise for who God is and thanksgiving for what God has done);
- Confession (prayers for forgiveness);
- Intercession (prayers for others), and
- Petition (prayers for oneself).

Keep on hand a variety of pencils, pens, markers and other art supplies.

Step 2: Throughout the day (or if that is not possible, at the end of the day) write, draw, doodle, paint or make a collage of pictures and symbols as your prayers. Words are optional). Offer at least one prayer-image for each heading.

20. Canticle of the Sun

PURPOSE: USE ST. FRANCIS' CANTICLE AS A PRAYER FOR THE WELL-BEING OF CREATION

Also known as "Canticle of the Creatures," this song by the 12th century saint will guide your prayers of praise and intercession for God's creation today.

Most high, all powerful, good God,
Yours are the praises, the glory, the honor, and all blessings.
To you alone, most high, do they belong,
And no one is worthy to mention your name.

Praise be to you, my Lord, through all your creatures,
especially through my Brother Sun,
who brings the day; and you give light through him.
And he is beautiful and radiant in all his splendor!
Of you, most high, he bears the likeness.

Praise be you, my Lord, through Sister Moon
and the stars; in heaven you formed them
clear and precious and beautiful.

Praise be you, my Lord, through Brother Wind,
and through the air, cloudy and serene,
and every kind of weather through which
You give sustenance to your creatures.

Praise be you, my Lord, through Sister Water,
which is very useful and humble and precious and chaste.

Praise be you, my Lord, through Brother Fire,
through whom you light the night, and he is beautiful
and playful and robust and strong.

Praise be you, my Lord, through Mother Earth,
who sustains us and governs us and who produces
varied fruits with colored flowers and herbs.

Praise be you, my Lord,
through those who give pardon for your love,
and bear infirmity and tribulation.

Blessed are those who endure in peace
for by you, most high, they shall be crowned.

Praise be you, my Lord,
through our Sister Bodily Death,
from whom no one can escape.
Woe to those who die in mortal sin.

Blessed are those whom death will
find in your most holy will,
for the second death shall do them no harm.

Praise and bless my Lord,
and give God thanks
and serve God with great humility.

There are a variety of ways to do this exercise:
- After each stanza pause to offer one prayer of praise and one prayer of intercession for different aspects of creation.
- After each stanza offer a prayer of confession for how we have violated that aspect of creation.
- Take a walk and offer this prayer as a way to frame your thoughts during your walk.

21. Praying Psalm 37:4

PURPOSE: TO EXPRESS YOUR DESIRES TO GOD

Psalm 37:4: "Take delight in the Lord and God will give you the desires of your heart."

Step 1: Say silently several times: "Take delight in the Lord" and center your thoughts on God, meditating on the attributes of God. What is the one characteristic of God that comes to the forefront of your thinking?

Step 2: Then, say silently several times: "and God will give me the desires of my heart." Ask yourself: What do I desire? Then ask yourself: Do these desires express some deeper needs I have?

Step 3: Finally, using the characteristic identified in Step 1 as a name for God, offer the following prayer: "[your name for God], I surrender my desires to you." For example, if the characteristic is divine power, you might pray: "Strong God, I surrender my desires to you."

22. Prayer Walk

PURPOSE: A PRAYER USING YOUR BODY TO EXPERIENCE GOD'S PRESENCE

Today, take a walk and pray while you walk.

There are a wide variety of ways to pray while you walk. You can use one of the previous prayer exercises while you walk.

You can use a variation of the "Lectio Divina" while you walk by paying close attention to the sights and sounds and smells as ways for encountering God.

Another form of walking prayer is the labyrinth. A labyrinth is an ancient practice of following a spiraling path that leads to a center and then winds back out to the place where you started.

23. "Here I Am" Prayer

PURPOSE: A BEGINNER'S PRAYER FOR SILENT MEDITATION

This prayer was developed by the Russian Orthodox Archbishop Anthony Bloom in his book "Beginning to Pray." Teresa Blythe adapted it below:

Step 1: Resolve to be in prayer for at least 5 minutes without distractions (or longer, if you feel up to it).

Step 2: Be seated and say to yourself, "Here I am seated, doing nothing. I will do nothing for 5 minutes."

Step 3: Begin noticing your own bodily presence—how your body feels next to the chair, how your feet feel against the floor. Relax your body. Notice what you feel inside.

Step 4: Now notice the presence of all that is around you. Say to yourself, "Here I am in the presence of the room (or wherever you are)." Be aware of the objects, creatures and happenings around you. Just be present and silent in your environment. Relax even more.

Step 5: Now say to yourself, "Here I am in the presence of God." Repeat silently to God, "Here I am." Stay in that moment until the allotted time comes to an end.

24. Paraphrase The Lord's Prayer

PURPOSE: EXPLORE DIFFERENT WAYS TO UNDERSTAND THE LORD'S PRAYER

Take each line of the Lord's Prayer and put it into your own words. Feel free to expand or change the words and phrases in new ways (for example, instead of "Our Father" try "Our Mother"). Spend the day thinking about the different ways you can paraphrase each line. At the end of the day, write down your version of the Lord's Prayer.

25. Hymn for the Day

PURPOSE: USE MUSIC AS A FORM OF PRAYER

Today, select a hymn or a number of hymns and sing or listen to them as your prayers. There are several ways this can be done:
- Select one hymn and sing or recite it at various intervals throughout the day.
- Sing a hymn at the beginning of your day and another hymn at the close of the day.
- Set aside a specified time to sit with a hymnal and sing various hymns.
- Set a hymnal in your kitchen and sing various hymns while you cook.
- Listen to recordings of hymns.

26. Prayers for the Dead

PURPOSE: TO REMEMBER AND GIVE THANKS FOR LOVED ONES WHO HAVE PASSED AWAY

Step 1: Make a list of persons who have died in the past year.

Step 2: Using this intercession from the "The United Methodist Book of Worship," remember each person by name:

Eternal God, you have shared with us the life of [*name(s)*].

Before *he/she/they* was ours, *he/she/they* was yours.

For all that [*name(s)*] has given us to make us what we are,

    for that of *him/her/them* which lives and grows in each of us,

    and for *his/her/their* life that in your love will never end,

    we give you thanks.

As now we offer [*name(s)*] back into your arms.
    Comfort us in our loneliness,
    strengthen us in our weakness,
       and give us courage to face the future unafraid.
Draw those of us who remain in this life closer to one another;
       make us faithful to serve one another,
       and let us know the peace and joy which is eternal life through Jesus Christ our Lord.
Amen.

27. Pushing Your Buttons

PURPOSE: A SELF-EXAMINATION AS TO WHY SOMETHING OR SOMEONE BOTHERS YOU

At noon and at the end of the day:

Step 1: Center yourself in the presence of God through an extended period of silence. Become aware that the Spirit is working in you to reveal to you what you need to learn and know.

Step 2: Ponder these questions:
- Why does this bother me?
- What memories or images from my past does it invoke?
- What sin does it tempt me to commit? (Is it a sin?)
- What different perspective does it invite me to consider?
- What new attitude or action does it invite me to take up?

Step 3: Close with an extended period of silence. At the end of the silence pray: "Lord, into your hands I commit my spirit. Amen." Let go of all intrusive thoughts and perseverations on the issue/persons.

28. Materialist Meditation

PURPOSE: REFLECT ON THE INTERSECTION BETWEEN ONE'S FAITH AND ONE'S FINANCES

Step 1: Read Matthew 6:24.

Step 2: Review your spending on all non-essential things over the past month. How do you define what is non-essential? What does this say about what you take delight in?

Step 3: Review all your giving, investing and savings. What does this say about the desires of your heart?

Step 4: End your time of meditation by reading Matthew 6:25 and 33.

Lay your hands on the device with which you keep your financial records (e.g. a checkbook, a folder, an app) and offer this prayer: "O God, all that I have is yours. You are in control; I am your servant. Thank you for all you have given and all you will give. Amen."

29. Wandering Prayer

PURPOSE: TO FOLLOW EVERY THOUGHT AND FEELING AS IT LEADS TO GOD

Often we think of prayer as a task of controlling our physical and mental distractions so we can say the rights words. In this exercise you are to do the opposite. Let your mind wander in the presence of God. Do not fight or try to control your thoughts and feelings and do not try to empty yourself. Instead, just go with the flow of all you think and feel with the intention of noticing it all in the presence of God so you may hear God through these sensations and thoughts.

Step 1: Find a comfortable position to sit for at least 10 minutes. Make sure you will not be distracted. If needed, set a timer to ring when this time is up.

Step 2: Begin by reading Psalm 19:14: "Let the words of my mouth and the meditations of my heart be acceptable to you, O Lord, my rock and my redeemer." Express to God your longing to experience God in this prayer.

Step 3: Let go of expectations and simply breathe. Exhale slowly, allowing each breath to find its own rhythm.

Step 4: Be attentive to your body. Do not try to control or avoid any irritations or feelings (such as needing to itch). Remind yourself that your body is in the presence of God and listen for how God might be speaking to you through these physical sensations. Be attentive to your thoughts. Let the random thoughts go through your mind. Do not dwell on them or try to suppress them. Remember that your heart and mind are in the presence of God, and imagine all these thoughts and feelings laid on the altar of God.

Step 5: When your time in prayer has come to a close, express your gratitude to God.

30. Moving to The Lord's Prayer

PURPOSE: TO EXPERIENCE THE LORD'S PRAYER THROUGH MOVEMENT

Begin by bringing your hands together, palm to palm, with fingers spread and touching each other. With your hands still together, slowly touch your forehead, lips, and heart, saying, "In the name of the blessed Holy Trinity." Then cross your arms over your chest and bow.

Now pray the Lord's Prayer (reciting or singing a cappella or to recorded music) while following these movements:
- "Our Father, who art in heaven, hallowed be thy name." (Raise arms with palms open in praise to God.)
- "Thy kingdom come, thy will be done on earth as it is in heaven." (Lower your arms outstretched to offer the world to God.)
- "Give us this day our daily bread." (Cup your hands

and touch your mouth.)

- "Forgive us our trespasses as we forgive those who trespass against us." (Lower your cupped hands over your heart.)
- "Lead us not into temptation but deliver us from evil." (Lower your hands to your sides.)
- "For thine is the kingdom and the power and the glory forever. Amen." (Raise arms with palms open in praise to God.)

31. Write Your Own Psalm

PURPOSE: USE WRITING TO EXPRESS YOUR PRAYER

Step 1: Decide what kind of psalm you want to write. Here are several examples from the book of Psalms in the Bible:
- Communal lament — 58;
- Individual lament — 3;
- Communal thanksgiving — 107;
- Individual thanksgiving — 116;
- Praise — 100;
- National — 72;
- Covenant — 50, and
- Wisdom — 1.

Step 2: Read samples of the type of psalm you want to write.

Step 3: Before writing, hold your palms upward on the table. Ask the Holy Spirit to inspire you, and dedicate your words to God's glory. Begin writing.

Step 4: When you are finished writing, read your psalm aloud.

32. Peace Prayer

PURPOSE: THE PRAYER OF ST. FRANCIS EXPRESSES OUR COMMITMENT TO BE GOD'S INSTRUMENTS OF PEACE IN THE WORLD. TODAY, USE THIS PRAYER TO FOCUS YOUR INTERCESSIONS FOR WORLD PEACE

Step 1: Research international conflicts. Include those conflicts that do not make the headlines as well as the well-known problems around the world.

Step 2: Offer to God each conflict by naming the place and the groups or individuals involved, asking for God to bring a just and lasting resolution to the conflicts.

Step 3: Pray, sing or listen to a recording of the Prayer of St. Francis:

> Lord, make me an instrument of thy peace;
> where there is hatred, let me show love;
> where there is injury, pardon;
> where there is doubt, faith;

where there is despair, hope;
where there is darkness, light;
and where there is sadness, joy.

O Divine Master,
grant that I may not so much seek
to be consoled as to console;
to be understood, as to understand;
and to be loved, as to love.

For it is in giving that we receive;
it is in pardoning that we are pardoned,
and it is in dying that we are born to eternal life.

33. Reconciliation By Water or Fire

PURPOSE: A RITUAL FOR THE CONFESSION OF SIN AND ASSURANCE OF FORGIVENESS

Two of the biblical symbols for the Holy Spirit are fire and water. Today's exercise is a ritual that expresses our confession of sin and the assurance of forgiveness that the Spirit gives us. Sometimes we need a ritual, in addition to the words of our prayer, to alleviate the burden of guilt we are carrying for our mistakes. There are two ways to do the ritual — one with fire and the other with water.

Step 1: Get some water or start a fire.

Step 2: Pray, "Lord, send your Spirit to cleanse me. May Christ make me a living sacrifice so that in every place I may praise you and proclaim your loving compassion, through Jesus Christ my Lord. Amen."

Step 3: Read Psalm 51.

Step 4: Confess your sins. If using water, write them on your hand with washable ink or state them aloud. If using fire, write them on a piece of paper.

Step 5: Symbolize the forgiveness for and freedom from sin God offers you. If using water, wash your hands and other body parts that symbolize the sins. If using fire, burn your list of sins.

Step 6: Read, "Hear the good news: Christ died for me while I was yet a sinner; that proves God's love for me. In the name of Jesus Christ I am forgiven. Glory to God. Amen."

Step 7: Resist the urge to keep rethinking and rehashing your guilt.

34. Audiebant Divina

PURPOSE: LISTEN TO GOD THROUGH MUSIC

Like a lectio divina, this "divine listening" uses music to hear the voice of God.

Step 1: Select a recorded song. (It does not need to be sacred or religious music; rather, it is any music that stirs your heart.)

Step 2: Listen to the song. Pay attention to the word or musical phrase that catches your attention. Do not analyze it or try to interpret it.

Step 3: Listen to the song a second time. Ask yourself, "What does this reveal about God?" Ponder the question for a few minutes.

Step 4: Listen to the song a third time. Ask yourself, "What does God want me to do or to be?" Ponder the question for a few minutes.

Step 5: With an awareness of God's presence, begin to pray.

35. Meditation on an Image

PURPOSE: LOOK FOR GOD THROUGH THE AID OF AN IMAGE OR AN OBJECT

All religions include the practice of meditation. The word "meditation" comes from the Greek *melete* that means "study," "care" or "exercise," and denotes a disciplined exercise that fosters listening to and intimacy with God.

Step 1: Choose a time of day that allows for ample time (for example, 30 minutes) and no distractions.

Step 2: Choose an image or object as your focal point for meditation related to one of Jesus' statements in the Gospel of John:

- Water, either flowing or in a bowl or glass (4:10);
- Bread (6:35, 38);
- Candle (8:12);
- Towel and basin or soap (13:5);
- Plant (15:1), or

- Cross (19:17).

Step 3: As you begin, sit in a comfortable position.

Step 4: Quiet your mind from other thoughts and begin breathing in a slow rhythm.

Step 5: Focus on the object or image. What is God revealing to you through it? What is God saying to you out of the silence?

Step 6: As you end your meditation, sit quietly and take time to refocus on your surroundings. You may want to close with a prayer, such as the Lord's Prayer.

36. Praying with Incense

PURPOSE: EXPLORE MEDITATION ON GOD'S GLORY AND GRACE

In scripture, incense expresses the prayers rising to God. The smell of incense and burnt offerings permeated the temple when Jesus went there for the last time and ran out the moneychangers in order to restore it to his Father's house of prayer (Matthew 21:13).

This exercise is divided into two sections of the same predetermined lengths of time to give ample opportunities for meditation (at least 5 minutes for each section). You may want to play appropriate music in the background.

Step 1: Light the incense and read Psalm 141:2: "My prayers rise like incense; my hands like the evening offering."

Step 2: Section One: Focus on the glory of God. Read Isaiah 6:3-4:

> "And one called to another and said: 'Holy, holy, holy

is the Lord of hosts; the whole earth is full of his glory.' The pivots on the thresholds shook at the voices of those who called, and the house filled with smoke."

Contemplate the majesty of God.

Step 3: Section Two: Focus on prayers of intercession for others rising before God. Read Malachi 1:11:

"For from the rising of the sun to its setting my name is great among the nations, and in every place incense is offered to my name, and a pure offering; for my name is great among the nations, says the Lord of hosts.

Imagine throughout the world prayers rising up to God. Offer your prayers for others.

Step 4: As you extinguish the incense, say "Holy, holy, holy is the Lord of hosts; the whole earth is full of his glory."

37. Divine Letter

PURPOSE: USE WRITING TO HELP YOU PRAY

Today, write a letter to God. Express the desires, questions and aspirations on your heart. This can be done as part of a journal. End your letter with these words: "Not my will but yours be done." (Luke 22:42).

Option: Seal the letter in an envelope, date it, and in three months open it and read it again as you consider how your prayers have or have not changed.

38. Five Senses Prayer

PURPOSE: TO BECOME AWARE AND CELEBRATE THE FULLNESS OF GOD'S PRESENCE

Step 1: Begin the day by reading.

Step 2: Throughout the day, focus on each of your five senses as a channel for experiencing God's presence:
- Where do you see God's majesty?
- Through whom do you hear God's truth?
- In what do you taste God's goodness?
- Who did God use to comfort you?
- When did you smell the beauty of God?

Step 3: At the end of the day, give God thanks for these divine encounters.

39. Fasting or Abstinence

PURPOSE: EXPERIENCE FASTING AS PRAYER

Fasting can be a form of prayer expressed through a temporary and intentional abstaining from food. In the Bible fasting was done for repentance (e.g. Joel 2:12-13) and intercession (e.g. Acts 14:23).

The purpose of fasting is twofold. Temporary abstinence helps the heart and mind focus on what is being prayed for. Also, the physical deprivation embodies the desires of the petitioner.

John Wesley recommended fasting on Thursday and Friday and it was a staple among early Methodists. It imitated the sequence of Jesus' Passion. There are many ways to fast besides this format. For more on fasting, read chapter four of Richard Foster's "The Celebration of Discipline." (At the end of this guidebook there is a pattern for Maundy Thursday and Good Friday.)

This exercise was designed to be done as a series of short reflections on the suffering and death of Jesus. Obviously you could spend a lot of time on each question and image, but this process will enable you to experience the entire story.

It is recommended to fast only from solid foods; continue to drink fluids and liquid meals (no alcohol). If you are unable to fast, this exercise can be done by abstaining from something else that is a normal part of your day that gives you comfort or pleasure.

Step 1: Select a specific day and time for your fast.

Step 2: Select a specific topic or theme on which to meditate and pray while you are fasting.

Step 3: Select specific scripture readings and other writings to guide your reflections.

Step 4: Bring your fast to an end with a song, a prayer of thanksgiving, and a simple meal.

40. Day of Simplicity, Silence, and Light

This exercise can be done any time but it was designed especially for "Holy Saturday." The day before Easter, "Holy Saturday" marks that period in the Passion story after Jesus is dead and descends into hell. It is a day of quiet simplicity prior to the great celebration of the resurrection on Easter morning.

Let today be a day of simplicity and solitude. Let it be a "down" day that is unrushed. Minimize all sources of media. Unclutter the mind and simplify your tasks, doing only what is necessary. At the close of the day do the following spiritual exercise in anticipation of Easter.

NIGHT MEDITATION ON THE LIGHT

PURPOSE: EXPLORE THE MEANING OF THE LIGHT

OF GOD

Light is a potent symbol in scripture that reveals various dimensions of God and Christ. This exercise explores those meanings. It can be combined with other prayer exercises.

Step 1: Set aside ample time free from distractions. Predetermine the amount of time you will spend.

Step 2: Light a candle. Allow your breathing to become slow and rhythmic as you set aside your mental distractions.

Step 3: As you watch the light, ponder the significance of its meaning about God and Christ. You can either:

- Allow your mind to wander with the image and let the Spirit reveal to you various meanings.

OR

- Read at various intervals these scripture verses and contemplate what they mean to you:
    - Then God commanded, "Let there be light"—and light appeared (Genesis 1:3).
    - The people who walked in darkness have seen a great light (Isaiah 9:2).
    - The light shines in the darkness, and the darkness has never put it out (John 1:5).
    - Jesus said, "I am the light of the world. Whoever follows me will have the light of life and will never walk in darkness." (John 8:12).
    - You are the source of all life, and in your light we see light (Psalm 36:9).
    - You are like light for the whole world....In

the same way your light must shine before people, so they will see the good things you do and praise your Father in heaven (Matthew 5:14-16).
- Your word is a lamp to guide me and a light for my path (Psalm 119:105).
- Wake up, sleeper, and rise from death, and Christ will shine on you (Ephesians 5:14).
- For the darkness is passing away, and the real light is already shining (1 John 2:8).
- If we love others we live in the light, and so there is nothing in us that will cause someone else to sin (1 John 2:10).

41. Lenten Supplemental Exercises

ASH WEDNESDAY MEDITATION

PURPOSE: EXPLORE THE MEANING OF ASH WEDNESDAY

Ash Wednesday launches the season of Lent by reminding us of our brokenness and mortality so we can humbly participate in God's transformative grace that prepares us for the celebration of Easter. In addition to attending one of the Ash Wednesday services, begin the season with the following meditation based on two different ways to translate Job 42:3 and 6.

Step 1: If you attend an Ash Wednesday service, do steps two through four during the imposition of the ashes. If you are unable to attend a service, place some ashes or dirt in your hand.

Step 2: [Mortality] Read Job 42:3 and 6:

"I have uttered what I did not understand, things too wonderful for me, which I did not know...Therefore I retract my words, and I am comforted concerning dust and ashes (i.e. my limitations)."

Pause for a moment and consider your mortality — your limitations and aspirations as a person who is both created in the image of God and is a creature among all other creatures.

Step 3: [Repentance] Read Job 42:3 and 6: "I have uttered what I did not understand, things too wonderful for me, which I did not know...Therefore I despise myself, and repent in dust and ashes (i.e. my sins)."

Pause for a moment and remember your sins. Ask for God's forgiveness.

Step 4: As you wash the ashes or dirt off your hands, give God thanks for your place in God's creation and for the forgiveness you have received.

A PATTERN FOR FASTING ON MAUNDY THURSDAY AND GOOD FRIDAY

This exercise was designed to be done as a series of short reflections on the suffering and death of Jesus. Obviously you could spend a lot of time on each question and image, but this process will enable you to experience the entire story.

This is a fast only from solid foods; continue to drink fluids and liquid meals. It begins after your meal on Thursday evening, the night of Jesus' Last Supper, and concludes Friday at 3 p.m. when Jesus died. At various intervals throughout the fast meditate on these events in Jesus' last hours.

If you are unable to fast this exercise can be done by

abstaining from something else that is a normal part of your day that gives you comfort or pleasure.

THURSDAY EVENING (after eating dinner)
Garden of Gethsemane
- "Father, if you are willing, remove this cup from me; not my will but yours be done." (Luke 22:42)
    - Surrender to God's will. What is the "cup" you do not want to pick up?
    - Imagine God helping you drink the cup like a mother helping a toddler with a cup.
- "Why are you sleeping?" (Luke 22:46)
    - Sins of omission. How have I fallen asleep in my commitment to Christ?
    - Imagine God trying to wake you up.
- "Is it with a kiss that you are betraying the son of man?" (Luke 22:48)
    - Sins of commission. How have I betrayed Christ in thought, word or deed?
- "Put your sword back, for all who live by the sword shall perish by the sword." (Matthew 26:52)
    - What violence is in my heart, my words, and my actions?
    - What systems of violence do I tacitly support with my lifestyle, outlook or spending?
    - Pray for the victims of violence.

From Gethsemane to the Palace of the High Priest
- "The High Priest stood up and said, 'Have you no answer to these charges?' But Jesus was silent."

(Matthew 26:62-3)
- Why didn't Jesus answer him?
- "I put you under oath before the living God; tell us if you are the Messiah, the Son of God." (Matthew 26:3)
  - Imagine what the power of Jesus, the anointed one of God, would look and sound like.
  - Let these thoughts be your last ones as you drift off to sleep.

FRIDAY MORNING
In the Courtyard
- "Before the cock crows you will betray me three times." (Matthew 26:75)
  - Pray that God will give you the strength to resist the temptation to deny or ignore Christ today.

From Caiaphas to Pilate
- "Are you the king of the Jews?" (Matthew 27:11)
  - How is Jesus Christ the ruler of my life?
  - What political and economic forces operate in opposition to the teachings of Jesus?

From Pilate to Herod
- "He questioned him at some length but Jesus gave him no answer." (Luke 23:9)
  - When have I demanded that Christ answer me?
  - When is Christ silent in my life?

From Herod to Pilate

- "Release Barabbas for us!" (Luke 23:18)
    - When have I placed my hopes and desires in someone or something other than Christ to free me?
    - What guilt would I rather live with than face Jesus Christ in my life?

The Sentencing
- "His blood be on us and our children." (Matthew 27:25)
    - How am I "responsible" for the death of Jesus?

The Torture
- Imagine the physical pain Jesus endured.
- Imagine the mental anguish Jesus endured.
- Pray for prisoners of conscience around the world. For more information go to www.amnestyusa.org or www.persecution.com.

The Way to Golgotha
- "They laid the cross on Simon of Cyrene and made him carry it behind Jesus." (Luke 23:26)
    - How can we carry the cross of Christ today?
- "Daughters of Jerusalem, do not weep for me, but weep for yourselves and for your children." (Luke 23:28)
    - Grieve and lament the injustice and exploitation of women and children in our world today.

FRIDAY, NOON TO 3 P.M.
The Crucifixion

- "Father, forgive them, for they know not what they do." (Luke 23:34)
    - Imagine yourself in the role of:
        - the mocking soldiers;
        - the skeptical criminal, and
        - the mourning women.
    - Confess all your sins and ask God to forgive you.
    - Think of everyone who has wronged you. Ask God to give you the grace to see them from Jesus' vantage point on the cross.
- "Jesus, remember me when you come into your kingdom." (Luke 23:42)
    - Use this phrase as a breath prayer.
    - Receive assurance through his words: "You will be with me in paradise."
- "My God, my God, why have you forsaken me?" (Matthew 47:46)
    - Remember those moments in your life when you have felt abandoned by God.
- "Father, into your hands I commend my spirit." (Luke 23:46)
    - Use this phrase as a breath prayer.
- "The curtain of the temple was torn in two." (Matthew 27:51)
    - Reconciliation: Praise God for all the ways Christ overcomes the barriers that separate us from God.

- "The earth shook, the rocks were split and the tombs were opened." (Matthew 27:51-2)
    - Victory: Praise God for:
        - the new life I have in Christ, and
        - the evil and injustice in the world that Christ is overcoming.
- "Truly, this man is the Son of God." (Mark 15:39)
    - At 3 p.m., repeat: "Truly he is the Son of God." Break the fast by eating a light meal.

About the Author

Darren Cushman Wood is the senior pastor of North United Methodist Church in Indianapolis, Indiana. He has served small and large, rural and urban United Methodist churches for over 30 years. He is a graduate of the University of Evansville and Union Theological Seminary.

He is the author of two books, hymns, and numerous articles. He is an adjunct professor of labor studies at Indiana University. He is married to Ginny and as of this writing they have three adult children and one grandchild.

www.ingramcontent.com/pod-product-compliance
Lightning Source LLC
Chambersburg PA
CBHW070302100426
42743CB00011B/2312